WESTMINSTER SCHOOLS

SMYTHE GAMBRELL
LIBRARY

PRESENTED BY

Patrick Thurman
1992

Alex Brissette

A DAY IN THE LIFE OF A
Stunt Person

by Stephen A. Wolf
Photography by Al Edwards

Troll Associates

All the stunts shown in this book are extremely dangerous and can be performed safely only by stunt professionals with proper stunt equipment and years of specialized training. No one should attempt to perform any stunt without proper training and professional safety measures.

Neither the Publisher nor the Author shall be liable for any damage which may be caused or sustained as a result of the conduct of any of the activities described in this book.

Library of Congress Cataloging-in-Publication Data

Wolf, Stephen, (date)
    A day in the life of a stunt person / by Stephen Wolf;
photography by Al Edwards.
        p.   cm.—(A Day in the life of)
    Summary: Describes the daily routine of a stunt man, including his
physical preparation for dangerous stunts and the equipment and
safety features involved.
    ISBN 0-8167-2222-6 (lib. bdg.)   ISBN 0-8167-2223-4 (pbk.)
    1. Stunt men and women—Juvenile literature. [1. Stunt men and
women. 2. Occupations. 3. Wolf, Stephen, 1963-   .] I. Edwards,
Al, 1959-   ill. II. Title. III. Series.
PN1995.9.S7W64 1991
792'.028'092—dc20   90-11101

The author and publisher would like to thank Emily Aronson, Diane Berkel, Jim
Bonney, Ross Clay, Austin Flynt, Sylvia Ipsen, Ed Levy, Lonny McDougal, Marika
Menutis, Sharon Moleski, Noel Rodriguez, Sheila Schmidt, Cherylanne Schreiner,
Amy Stiller, Eric Von Bleichen, Burt Wolf, Chouinard Company, and The Gately/
Poole Acting Studio for their generous assistance and cooperation.

Stephen Wolf is a stunt performer for motion pictures. In order to do stunt work, you have to be in excellent physical condition. This means getting enough sleep, eating a healthful diet, maintaining proper weight, and getting plenty of exercise. Four times a week Stephen starts his day at the gym.

The first step of Stephen's regular exercise routine is to stretch out so his muscles will be limber. If your muscles are tight when you exercise, you can easily hurt yourself. Stephen stretches his legs, arms, and abdomen muscles.

Stephen does sit-ups on the sit-up bar to strengthen his abdominal muscles. Then he moves to the weight machines where he can adjust the weights he lifts. These machines help build upper body strength, which is important for stunt work. Sometimes Stephen's stunts require long periods of hanging on cables, pulling ropes, or climbing.

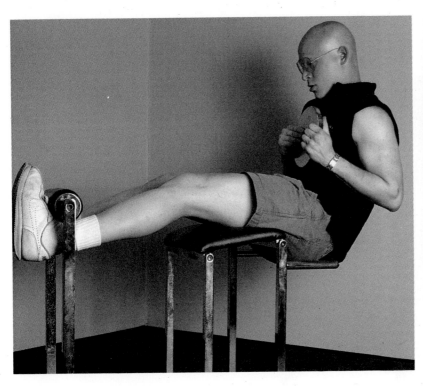

Occasionally stunt work requires underwater activities. To prepare for a stunt that will be performed later in the week, Stephen practices some scuba exercises in the pool. He also tests the two compressed-air regulators that he will be using to make sure they are in good condition for the stunt.

After his early-morning workout, Stephen goes to the movie set where he is working this week. His first stunt of the day will be a *box fall*, where he will fall off a building into special boxes made for stunt work. He discusses the setup for the stunt with his assistant, and they start building the boxes that will be needed.

To prevent injury, exactly the right number of boxes must be used, based on the height of the fall and Stephen's weight. Once the boxes are assembled, they are laid out over a large area called a *drop zone*. Stephen arranges the boxes in layers, which are tied together with rope. He puts a few flat boxes on top of the first layer, then adds a second layer of boxes and ties them securely.

Once all the stunt boxes are in place, layers of padding and a plastic tarp are draped over them. The layered boxes create a *crash pad* that will cushion Stephen's fall. The crash pad is set up like a giant balloon that will absorb the impact of the fall.

Paramedics must always be on the set when a stunt is being performed. Stephen shows the paramedic a diagram that explains exactly what the stunt will look like. He also explains how all the safety equipment works so the paramedics will immediately know if something is going wrong during the stunt.

Once the crash pad is fully set up in the drop zone, Stephen goes up to the roof. Yesterday, a fight scene was filmed where someone was supposedly thrown from the roof. When Stephen performs the fall today, he will dress in clothes that match the ones the actor was wearing. When the film is edited, it will look as though the whole scene had been shot at once.

Stephen spends several minutes looking down at the crash pad. It looks very small from the top of the building. He meditates for about ten minutes to help him relax. Before he can perform any stunt, his mind must be at peace so he can have total focus. Any distraction could be disastrous.

Even though the boxes will crush like giant marsh-mallows when Stephen hits them, he must still wear protective padding for every part of his body. He wears pads to protect his knees and elbows, and a special vest around his chest to prevent his lungs from overexpanding on impact. Once he has all his protective gear in place, Stephen puts on the ward-robe that matches the actor's clothing.

Stephen lies in the position where the actor was before he was supposedly thrown off the roof. He lets the director know that he is ready by giving him a signal with his hands. When the director says, "Action," Stephen counts down: "Three! Two! One! Ahhhhh!" and begins his drop.

Stephen shouts through his whole trip down to the ground. He turns his body around while he is in the air to make sure he lands on his back. It is important that he lands in the right position so he does not injure himself. Within seconds he hits the crash pad.

Stephen has hit the target dead center. Before he moves, he gives a thumbs-up to the crew to let them know that he is okay. Once they have received his signal, crew members can come to Stephen's aid to help him climb off the crash pad.

Stephen must perform the stunt two more times
to make sure the director gets the shots he wants.
After the stunt is completed for the third time,
Stephen breaks down his gear and goes home to
work on his next stunt of the day.

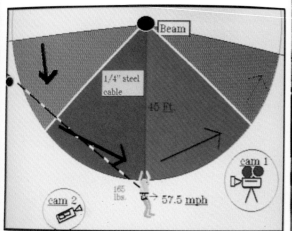

Stunt people often use computers to figure out how to do stunts. Stephen reviews a swinging stunt he will perform later that day. In the script, a hostage is tied to a long chain that is dangling from a ceiling beam. When the hostage is pushed from another beam, he swings across the room, dangling from the chain. The computer screen shows the best camera positions for filming the stunt.

After he has reviewed his plans on the computer, Stephen gets started on the swinging stunt. This stunt requires a lot of *rigging*, or setting up of cables and ropes. Since the safety equipment is not supposed to show in the film, Stephen's first step is to spray-paint the shiny metal rings called *carabiners* with black paint so they will blend into the dark background.

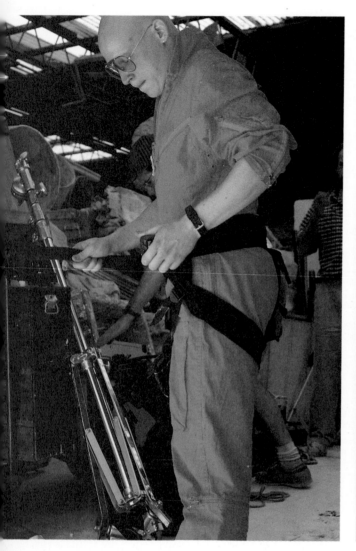 

To set up this stunt, Stephen will have to attach ropes and cables to beams that are 30 feet high. Since he will be working at dangerous heights, Stephen must wear harnesses like the ones worn by mountain climbers. One section of the harness is tied around his hips, and the other section goes around his chest.

Stephen attaches the top and bottom parts of the harness with the strong carabiners. Once his harness is put together, he gathers his gloves and equipment box and is ready to start rigging.

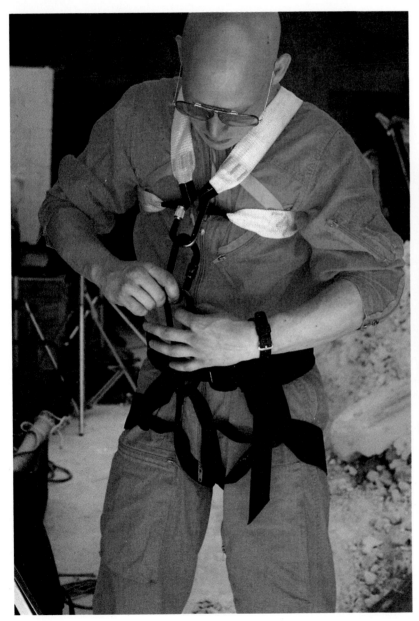

On the set the stunt coordinator, the chief rigger, and Stephen review where cables and ropes need to be attached to high beams. Setting up this stunt is more dangerous than performing it, so only a stunt person can work on the rigging. Stephen examines the area he will be preparing for the stunt.

A cable around the beam is attached to Stephen's harness to catch him if he should slip when he is working high up. He tests his harness, and then climbs up onto the beams. It is for jobs like these that Stephen needs as much upper body strength as possible.

Even though he is 30 feet up in the air with no safety net beneath him, Stephen moves around comfortably on the beams. He balances himself so he can sit upright on the beam to attach the rope, then he wraps his body around the beam so he can slide across and suspend the rope from the center.

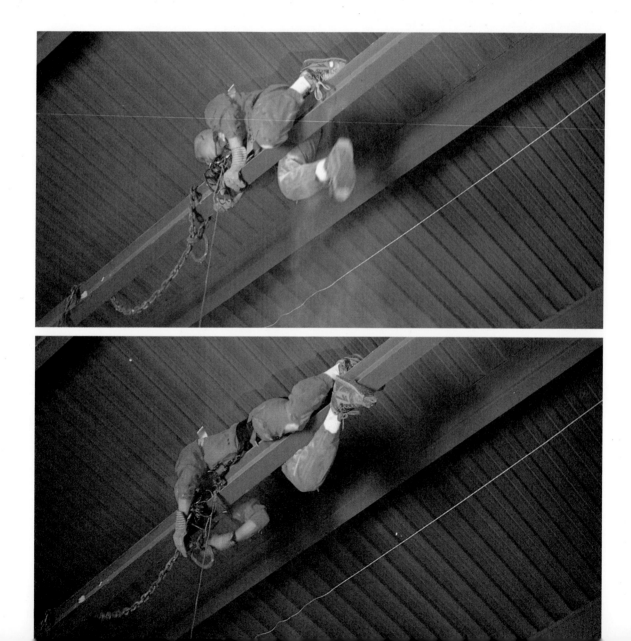

With a few hours to go before the stunt will be performed, Stephen comes down from his rigging and makes a phone call. He calls the paramedics to make sure they will be on the set before the filming begins. Although he takes every possible safety precaution when he does his stunts, accidents can still happen, so Stephen will not perform a stunt without paramedics being on the set.

Before he returns to the beams, Stephen must get more equipment from his rigging box. He makes some strong knots and attaches extra coils of rope to his harness. He needs to have the extra ropes at his disposal while he is up on the beams moving the cables around.

Once all the ropes and cables are in place, he checks each one visually from high above, then tests them from below by hanging and tugging on them vigorously. He must be absolutely sure that the cables will not slide around when he is swinging on them.

Once the gear is all set up, he goes to the makeup room to be made up for the stunt. A makeup artist makes Stephen look just like the actor he will be doubling for in this scene. The color of his wig and his skin tone must match the actor's so that when the film is seen, no one can tell that the actor did not do the stunt himself.

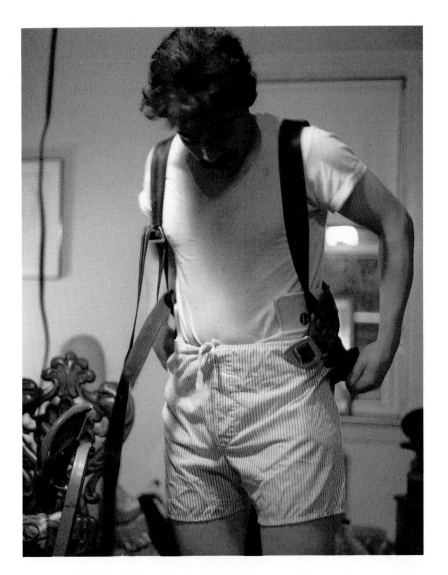

After he is made up, Stephen must put on specially designed harnesses that will not show underneath his costume. They are not as comfortable as the harnesses he wore while he was rigging. After his harnesses are secured, he can put on the same clothes that the actor was wearing when he filmed the rest of the scene.

Back on the set, the stunt coordinator attaches the harness under Stephen's clothing to the cables attached to the beams. Stephen is hauled up to the ceiling. When the crew is set and the director says "Action," one of the cables is let go, and Stephen drops down and swings quickly across the ground and back up into the air. The stunt has gone off successfully.

Although Stephen has finished his stunt work, his day is not over. Since much of his stunt work involves acting, he also attends classes for acting and movement techniques five times a week. Stephen says that often the acting is scarier than his stunt work.

At the end of a long and tiring day, Stephen relaxes at home. Often he watches action films and tries to figure out how the stunts were performed. He knows that tomorrow his day will be just as thrilling and challenging as anything he watches on television.